Let's Learn Sign Language Together!

ASL for Beginners and Early Readers

Written & Illustrated by

Rosa Padilla

Copyright © Rosa Padilla 2022
© ISBN: 9780998221021
All Rights Reserved.

"Elephant." The Columbia Encyclopedia, 6th ed. 22 Aug. 2017 http://www.encyclopedia.com.

"Koala." The Columbia Encyclopedia, Aug. 2017 http://www.encyclopedia.com.

"Moon." The Gale Encyclopedia of Science. Aug. 2017 http://www.encyclopedia.com.

"Oceans and Estuaries." Water; No Longer Taken For Granted. Aug. 2017 http://www.encyclopedia.com.

"Rose Hip." Gale Encyclopedia of Alternative Medicine. Aug. 2017 http://www.encyclopedia.com.

"Sun, Moon, and Earth." Science of Everyday Things. Aug. 2017 http://www.encyclopedia.com.

Printed in the United States of America

Copyright © 2022 by Rosa Padilla
© ISBN: 9780998221021

All Rights Reserved.

No part of this book may be reproduced or used in any manner without the prior written permission of the copyright owner.

For Information regarding permission, write to:

Rosa Padilla, P.O. Box 1303, Yonkers, NY, 10704

Psalm 119:2

I dedicate this book to all the children in the world!

This book belongs to:
_____

Copyright © 2022 by Rosa Padilla
© ISBN: 9780998221021

It's a great day to eat **apples**!
Apples are a sweet fruit.
Let's sign the letter **A**.

Baseball, basketball, and football are all sports played with different types of balls.
Let's sign the letter B.

Carrots are a healthy nutritious snack! **Carrots** start with the letter **C**. Let's sign the letter **C.**

Daisies are beautiful flowers.
Did you know that you can add daisy
leaves to your salad? There are
both enjoyable and appetizing,
let's sign the letter D.

Elephants are the largest living land mammal found in Africa and Asia!
Let's sign the letter **E**.

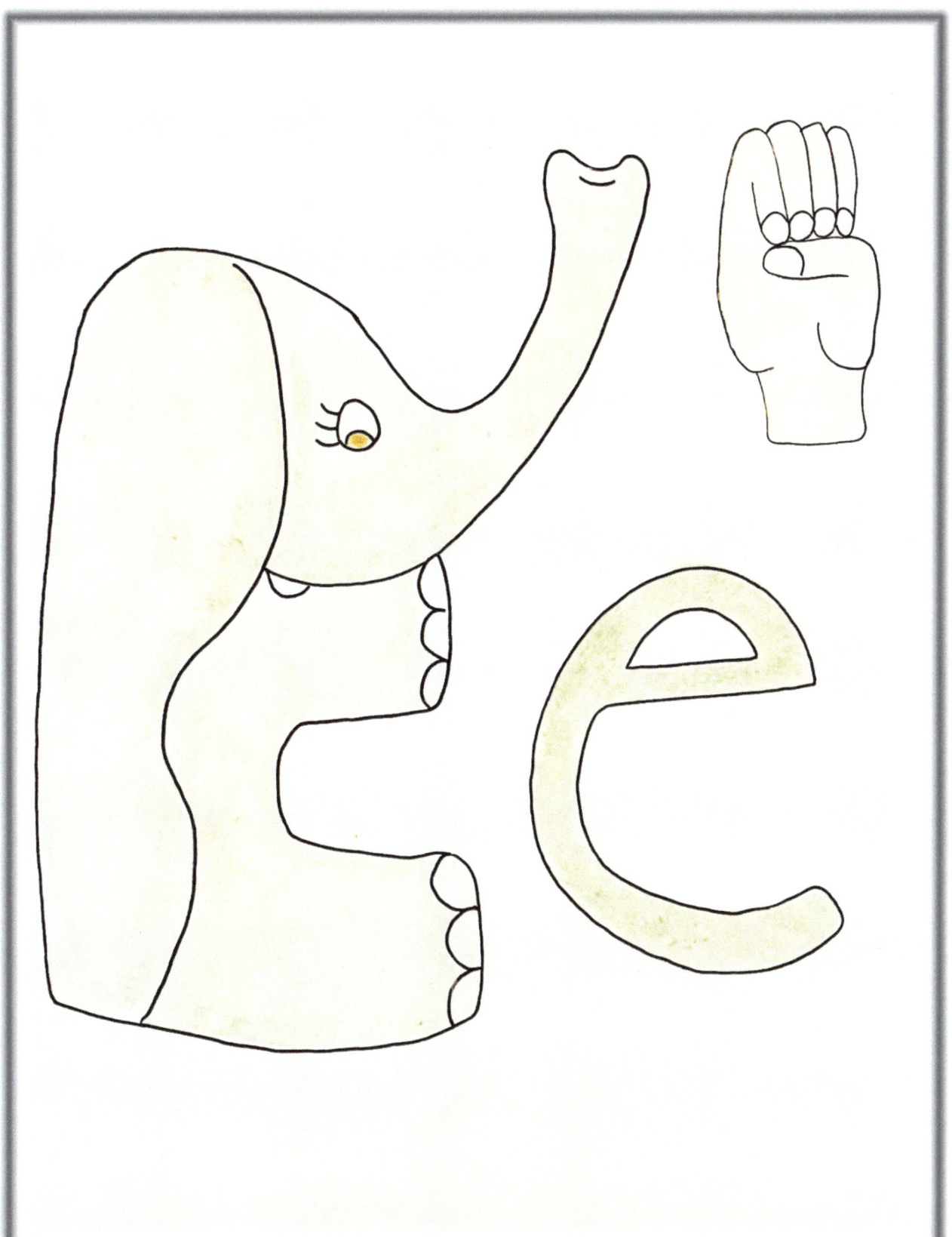

What kind of creatures do you see at the aquarium? If you guessed fishes, you are correct! Let's sign the letter F.

Globes are used to locate places such as: The United States of America, Australia, London, Rome, and Japan.
Let's sign the letter G.

On Valentine's Day,
you can make cards with **hearts** on them.
The word **heart** starts with the letter **H**.
Let's sign the letter **H.**

There are many flavors of ice cream: strawberry, chocolate, vanilla, and many more.
What are your favorite flavors?
Let's sign the letter I.

Jellyfish are unlike fishes in the sea because they don't have gills or scales. Also, Jellyfish are mostly composed of water.
Jellyfish start with the letter J.
Let's sign the letter J.

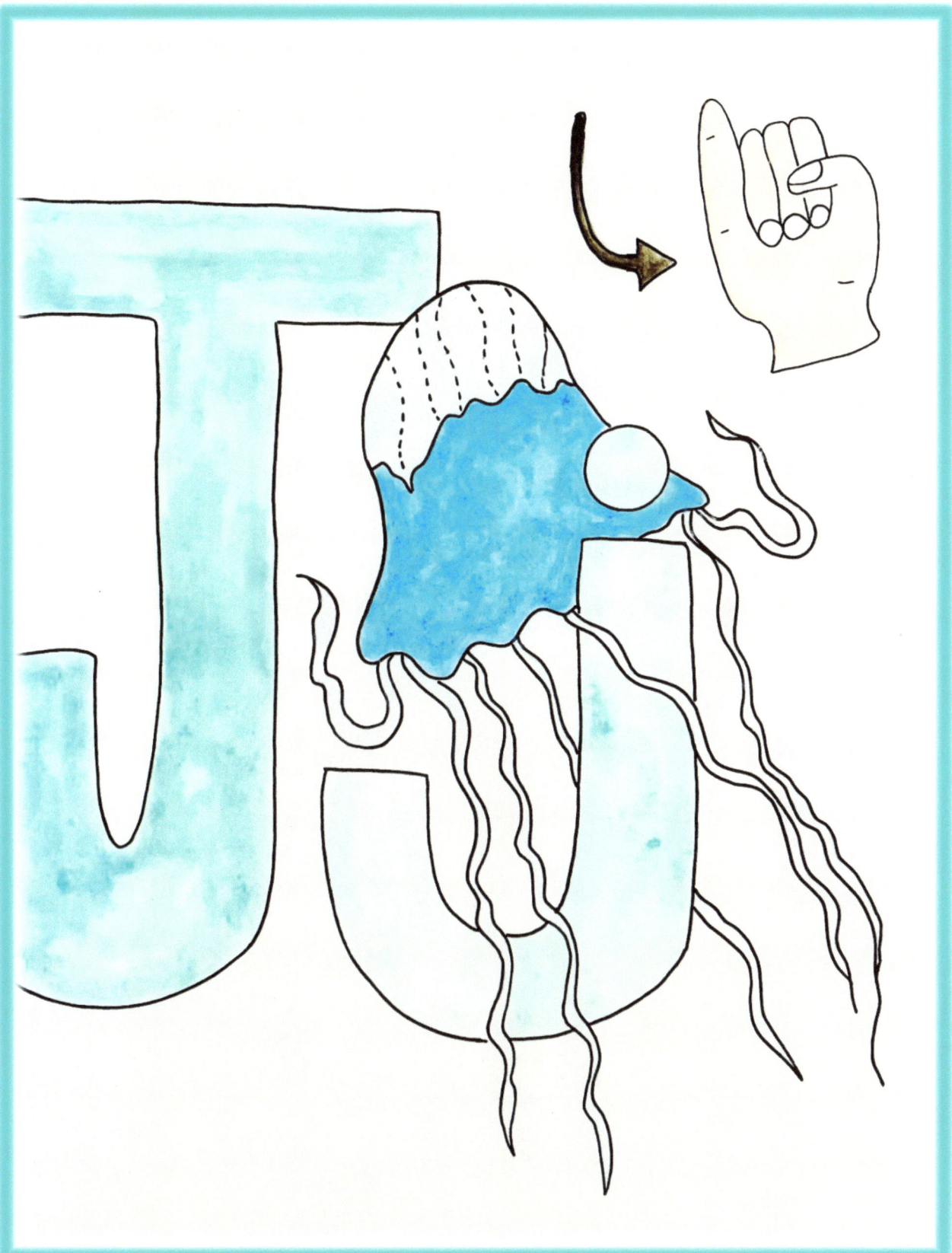

A baby Koala is called a "Joey."
Did you know that koalas have a
very particular diet?
Koalas eat eucalyptus leaves!
Let's sign the letter K.

Lions are carnivores from the cat family!
Lions roar loud and live in large groups known as, "prides."
Let's sign the letter L.

Here are some fun facts about the Moon!
There are several different moon phases.
Such as the crescent moon, new moon,
and a full moon.
Another name for moon is Luna?
Let's sign the letter M.

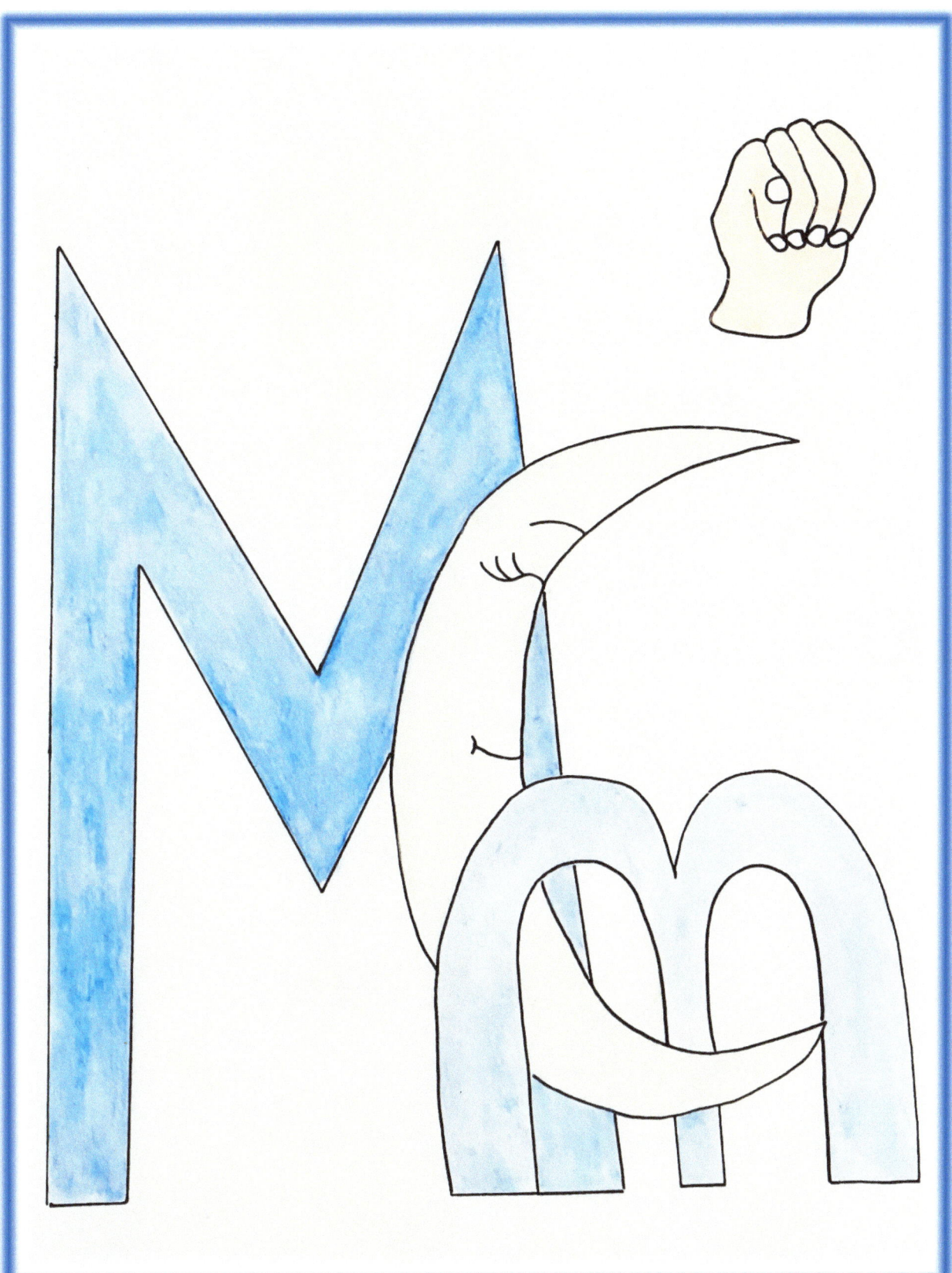

Musicians read different **notes** to play all types of instruments. Some instruments include, the piano, guitar, and the trumpet. Let's sign the letter **N**.

There are four subdivisions of oceans on planet Earth. Can you name all four?
1. Arctic 2. Atlantic 3. Indian 4. Pacific
Let's sign the letter O.

Pancakes are a great choice for a tasty breakfast in the morning.
Pancakes are also the topic of another book by Rosa Padilla,
titled "I Love **Pancakes**."
Let's sign the letter **P**.

The next letter in the alphabet is Q. The word quiet starts with the letter Q. Let's sign the letter Q.

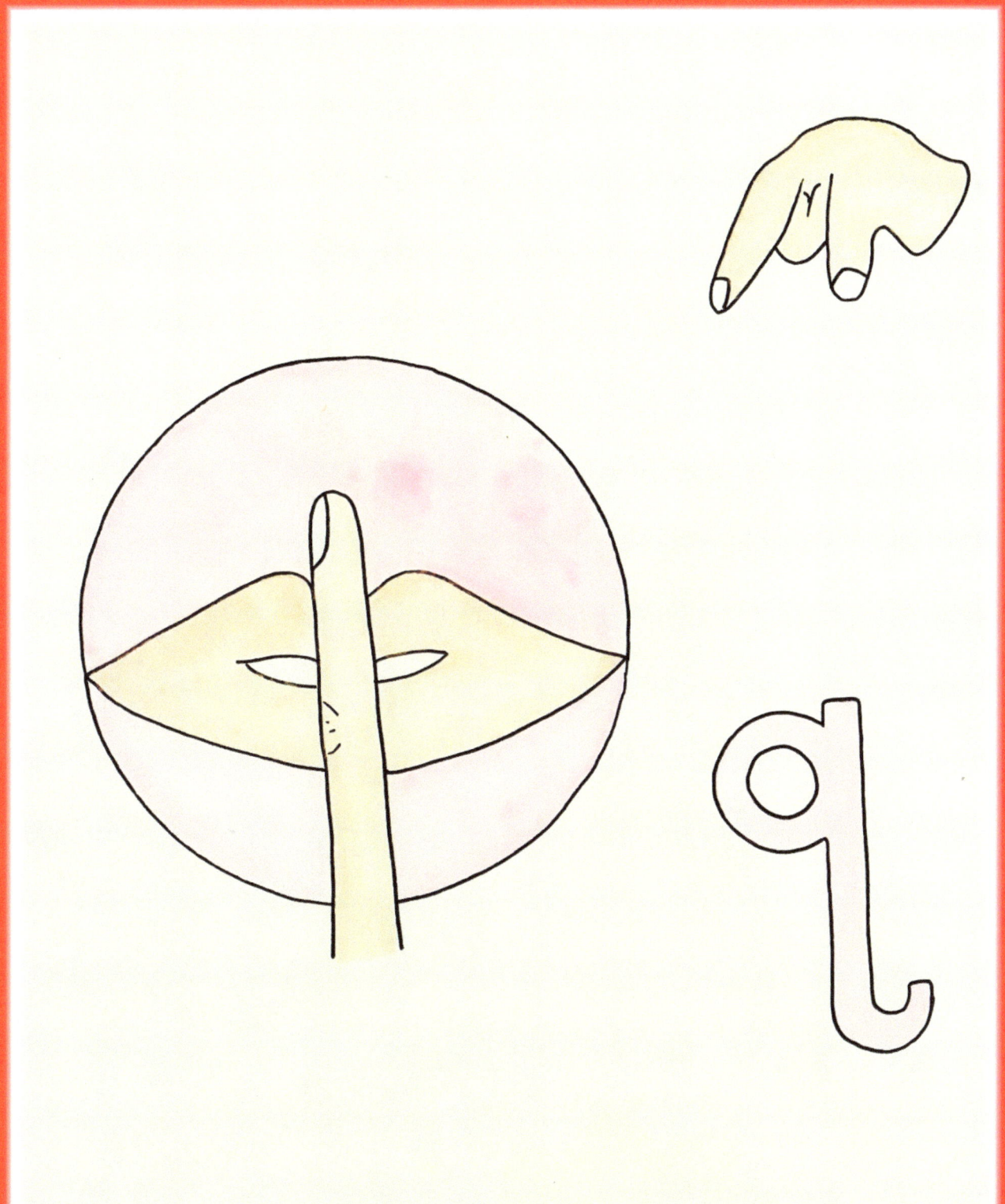

Roses are unique flowers.
Did you know that the rose hip
is from the fruit of a rose plant?
Rose hips also rich in vitamin C!
Let's sign the letter R.

Earlier we mentioned the moon,
but what about the sun?
Did you know that the sun is a star?
It is found at the center of the solar system!
Let's sign the letter S.

Turtles are very smart sea creatures that are often recognized by their shell.
Turtles begin with the letter T.
Let's sign the letter T.

The function of an **umbrella** is to cover, shade, and protect us from different types of weather.
Let's sign the letter **U**.

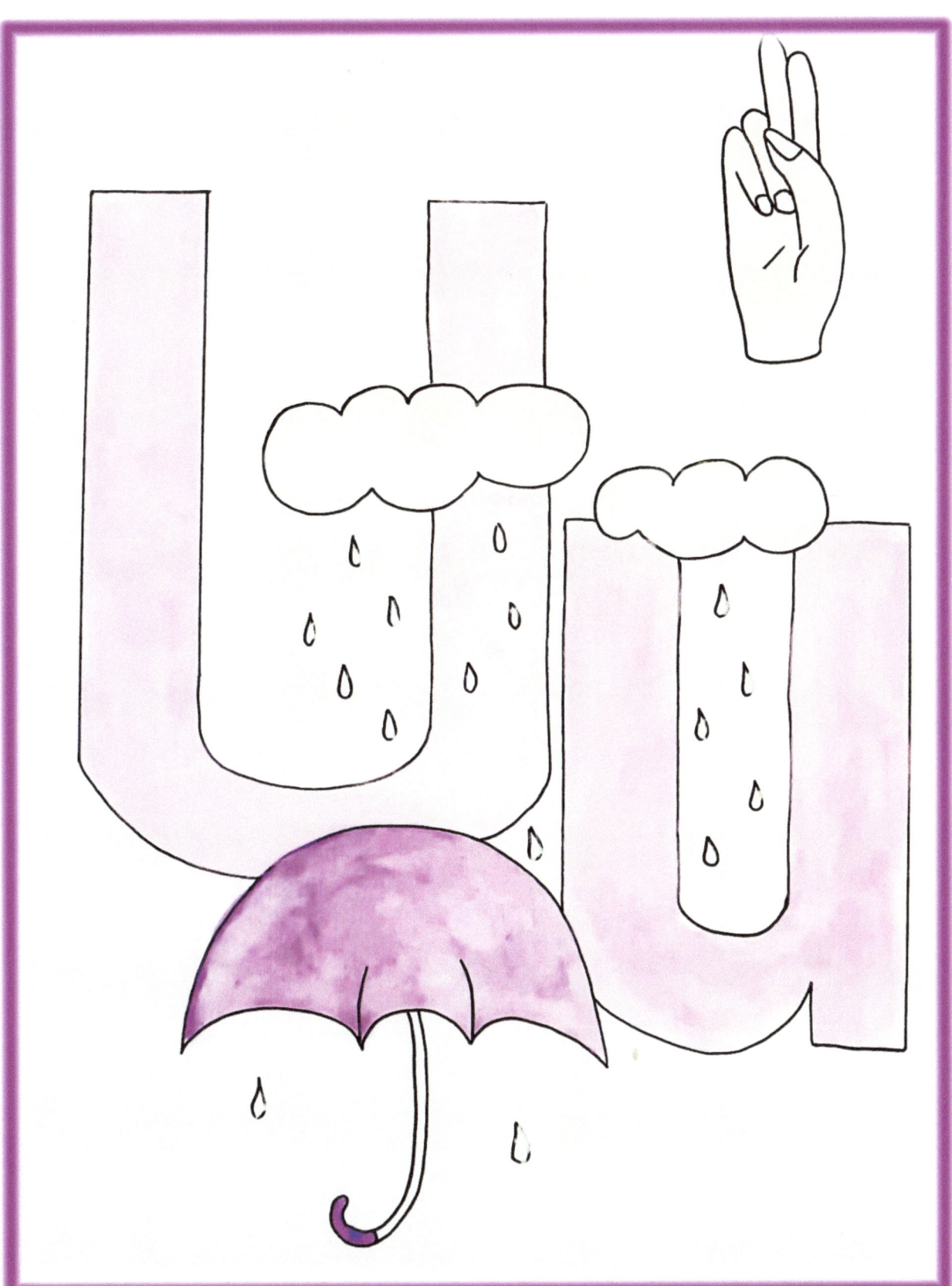

The **violin** is a wooden four string instrument.
Violin starts with the letter **V**.
Let's sign the letter **V**.

Watermelons are yummy and nutritious fruits. Do you like to eat watermelons?
Let's sign the letter W.

The letter X is the 24th letter in the alphabet. If you look on a treasure map usually the X is where you can find the gold or hidden treasure. X marks the spot! Let's sign the letter X.

A yo-yo is a toy that is fun to play with. Yo-yos rotate up and down, and can come in a variety of colors and sizes.
Let's sign the letter Y.

Z is the 26th letter in the alphabet.
Zucchini starts with the letter Z.
Zucchinis are sweet and savory.
You can make zucchini
spaghetti, zucchini fries and
zucchini muffins!
Let's sign the letter Z.

To the Reader:

I often think about how I can **INSPIRE** others.

How I can make others **SMILE** and **LAUGH**.

I write, illustrate, and **CREATE** books for everyone.

I **HOPE** this book will bring you **JOY**!

Sincerely,

Rosa Padilla

www.ingramcontent.com/pod-product-compliance
Lightning Source LLC
Chambersburg PA
CBHW040100160426
43193CB00002B/31